Timesaving Techniques 2
  Sewing Supplies 2
  Rotary Cutting Equipment 2
  Steps to Rotary Cutting Accuracy 3
  More Rotary Cutting Tips & Tricks 3
  Machine-Piecing Guidelines 4
  Sewing and Rotary Cutting Terms 4

Using Color Effectively 5
  Planning a Quilt: The Importance of
  Color, Value, and Contrast 5
  More Tips on Color 8

Heirloom Quilts 10
  Four-Patch & Nine-Patch 10
  Stars & Spinners 14
  March Pinwheels 18
  Bunkhouse Scraps 24
  Almost Amish 28

©2013, from *Rotary Heirloom Quilts* (AQS, 2002)

Almost Amish
page 28

TIMESAVING TECHNIQUES

The quilts in this book are designed for rotary cutting and quick piecing. Sewing strips, triangles, squares, rectangles, and other shapes together and cutting them into patchwork segments will allow you to make each of these heirloom quilts quickly and easily. Some of the shapes, such as wedges, will need to be rotary cut from dimensions listed on diagrams, or from templates provided in the project instructions. Below, you will find lists of general sewing supplies and rotary-cutting equipment you will need to make the quilts on the following pages, along with some of my favorite tips and hints for rotary-cutting and machine-piecing success.

Sewing Supplies

Sewing machine
Use a sewing machine that has a straight-stitch capability for all machine piecing.

Machine needles
Use a quilting or sharp embroidery machine needle for machine piecing. Change the needle in your machine after approximately 8 hours of sewing time.

Threads
Use high quality, 100-percent cotton or cotton-covered polyester all-purpose threads for machine piecing.

Seam ripper
Use a sharp seam ripper with a safety tip for removing seams.

Fabric scissors
Use sharp scissors for trimming seam allowances and clipping threads.

Marking tools
Light and dark removable fabric markers make it easy to see lines on almost any fabric. Experiment with scraps of fabric you plan to use in your quilt to determine which marking tools you like best.

Rotary Cutting Equipment

Rotary Cutters
Choose a rotary cutter that is comfortable and designed to be used in your dominant hand. There are now good tools designed for both right-handed and left-handed people. If you are ambidextrous, look for a rotary cutter that can be used in either hand. I like to keep one at my cutting table and one beside me at my sewing machine.

Blades
Sharp rotary-cutting blades make the cutting process a much more pleasurable experience. Dull blades result in gnawed, uneven edges (and frustrated quilters!). Change the blade in your rotary cutter often, and discard used blades safely so that no one can be accidentally injured by them.

Cutting Mats
My favorite rotary mat size is 24" x 36", with a marked grid on one side. I use a self-healing mat, because I believe the fabric clings to this type better. Consider purchasing more than one cutting mat; I own several that I use next to my sewing machine and take with me when I travel.

Acrylic Rulers
Look for accurate measurements that are easy to read on rotary rulers of any shape or size. For starters, select a 6" x 24" straight ruler and another ruler that measures 6" x 12". Look for rulers with marked lines indicating 45° and 60° angles, which can be used for cutting the triangles and wedge shapes in this book. Eventually you will acquire various rulers and triangles in different widths, lengths and shapes. Invest in them as you need them.

TIMESAVING TECHNIQUES

Steps to Rotary Cutting Accuracy

Preparing the fabric properly and using good rotary cutting tools will make your cutting more accurate and enjoyable. Follow these steps to ensure rotary-cutting success.

1. Start by straightening the grain of the fabric by pulling at opposite corners. First, pull in one direction and then in the opposite direction.

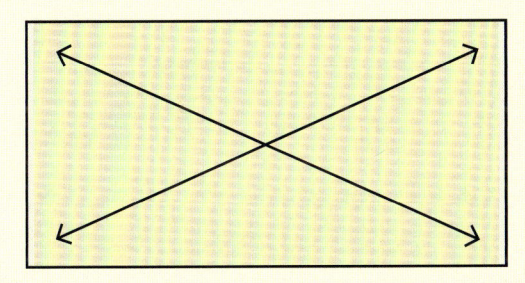

2. Fold the fabric once, placing the selvages together. The fabric needs to be flat and smooth for accurate rotary cutting.

3. Place the folded fabric along one of the horizontal lines on the cutting mat. The grid lines are important for ensuring straight cuts. Let the fabric extend to the right if you are right-handed, or to the left if you are left-handed.

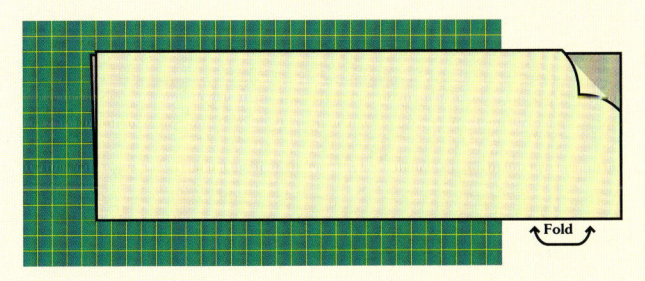

4. Lay a ruler along one of the vertical gridlines and on the horizontal line where the fold is placed. Slip the ruler over the raw edges of the fabric and realign the horizontal and vertical lines of the ruler with those on the mat. Open the rotary cutter blade, place it flush against the acrylic ruler, and press down firmly. Beginning on the mat, move the rotary cutter toward the fabric (away from you) and cut through the folded fabric with a single, clean motion. This first cut is to trim just enough of the fabric away to create a straight edge at the left side (or the right side, if you are left-handed).

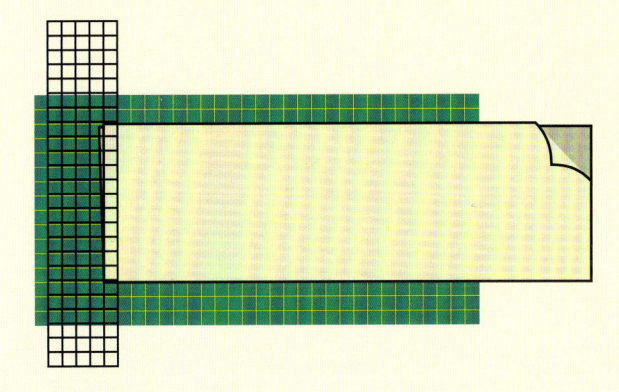

5. After trimming a straight edge, realign the fabric with the horizontal line on the mat, if necessary, and reposition ruler on the fabric at whatever strip width you wish to cut. Take note of the type and number of pieces you will need to cut for your quilt. Post this information close to your cutting table and refer to it often as you cut the pieces for your quilt. In this way, you will be more likely to cut only what you need. I'm always reminded of the carpenter's rule: "Measure twice – cut once!"

More Rotary-Cutting Tips & Tricks

After you've mastered the basics of rotary cutting, remember the following tips and tricks to ensure successful rotary cutting every time.

♦ Rotary cutters perform best and stay sharp longer when used on 100% cotton fabrics.
♦ Rotary cutters will cut up to twelve layers at a time. Experiment to determine the number of layers you are able to cut with accuracy.
♦ Do not make gestures with your hand while you are holding a rotary cutter—danger may lie ahead!
♦ Always keep your cutting mat on a flat surface. When you are not using it, store it flat and away from heat to avoid warping it.
♦ Pin a written identification label to each stack of cut strips and pieces for a quilt, including the binding strips, so there will be no confusion about strips or pieces of similar widths or sizes.

Machine-Piecing Guidelines

Here are some of my favorite tips and tricks for ensuring machine-piecing accuracy.

Know your sewing machine. Before making any of these quilts, take a minute to sew 2 scrap strips of fabric together to make sure that you are stitching an accurate ¼" seam allowance. Precise stitching is critical for making sure that your finished quilts will be the correct size. Inaccurate seam allowances can cause significant problems.

Know your own sewing habits. If you find that your seam allowance width is inconsistent, analyze the way you sit at your sewing machine and how it affects your piecing. For example, I tend to tip my head to one side as I sew, which can lead to slight variations in seam allowance widths. Becoming aware of your posture and personal sewing habits can help you make your machine piecing more accurate.

Sew all patchwork seam allowances with the right sides of the fabric together unless otherwise stated in the project instructions.

Press all seam allowances to one side and toward the darker fabric, unless otherwise indicated in the project instructions.

Sew border strips and binding strips together with 45-degree seams. Trim the excess fabric on the wrong side to ¼" from your stitching lines. Press these seam allowances open to avoid bulky areas in borders and bindings.

Press patchwork seam allowances on a very firm board, which will flatten the seams better than a softer surface.

To make the backing of a quilt, determine whether you want the seam(s) in the backing to be vertical or horizontal. Determine how many lengths of fabric you will need to sew together to create the backing. Trim the selvages before sewing the lengths of backing fabric together. Press the seam allowances open to avoid bulk in areas to be quilted.

The quilts in this book feature double-fold binding; the cut strip width is 2½".

Sewing and Rotary-Cutting Terms

Chain piecing: Sewing many of one type of unit in one continuous, long chain, without lifting the presser foot or cutting thread between units.

Finger-pressing: Opening a stitched seam allowance with your fingers and pressing the seam allowance flat with the balls of your fingers, taking care not to stretch or distort the fabric.

Strip piecing: Sewing long strips of fabric to each other or to previously sewn units.

Strip-sets: The combination of 2 or more sewn strips; strip-sets are then cut into smaller segments to create various units of patchwork.

Squaring blocks: Measuring and trimming pieced blocks so they will all be the same size. Do not trim away ¼" seam allowances.

USING COLOR EFFECTIVELY

Planning a Quilt:
The Importance of Color, Value, and Contrast

As Plato, the Greek philosopher, once stated, "composition consists of observing and depicting diversity within unity." As quiltmakers, we can take advantage of this concept of diversity within unity to plan beautiful quilt designs. Think of the patchwork units in a quilt as the source of unity throughout a design, and consider the unlimited number of possible color combinations as the diversity that each of us can bring to our own projects.

Appreciation and use of color and contrast are very individualistic. We each have the ability to use these elements of design with little or no formal training. Color attracts the eye and sets the mood of a quilt, but it is the contrast between lights and darks (color values) that defines the shapes in a quilt design. As you plan a quilt, think about how you want your quilt to look when it is finished, how you would like the various patchwork units of the design to flow together or be divided, and how you can use value to create a quilt that reflects your own unique preferences. Keep planning the design down to the smallest detail to create quilts that sparkle with energy and life.

Use color value, which is the lightness or darkness of a color, to determine the framework of your quilt. Start by asking yourself questions like these: In what parts of the quilt would you like to feature dark fabrics? Where should lighter values be used to highlight the design? Having a framework or "skeleton" of lights and darks, as in this MARCH PINWHEELS quilt, is a great way to create an effective quilt design, even before you begin to consider the element of color itself.

MARCH PINWHEELS
page 18

Create visual impact by allowing one color or value to dominate the quilt instead of spotting each color equally over the pattern design. Vary the shape, size, and even distance between the various colors, as shown in the ALMOST AMISH quilt on page 28. A quilt should appear balanced and unified. It should contain enough diversity to keep viewers interested as their eyes move across the surface of the quilt.

Create areas of focus within either the individual blocks or within the whole quilt design. At this stage of planning, you might consider rendering "lost and found" edges of the pattern. Another tactic might be to include an unexpected texture or accent color.

STARS & SPINNERS
page 14

USING COLOR EFFECTIVELY

Non-focus color and value areas of the quilt generally contain medium-valued fabrics, having little personality of their own. These fabrics are just as important as more dominant colors or values because they provide the background that supports the dominant colors and values, as you can see in the BUNKHOUSE SCRAPS quilt on pages 8 and 9. Even after color and visual texture are applied to a quilt design, the underlying skeleton of value can still be seen.

FOUR-PATCH & NINE-PATCH
page 10

More Tips on Color

Effective color use is an art rather than a science, and it is an art quilters learn and understand through experience and making quilts. You may have read a considerable amount about color theory and color harmonies on a color wheel. It is possible to earn a Ph.D. in the study of color theory, do post-graduate work on the same topic, and still find more to learn about color. The good news is that almost any color can be made to go with any other color, given the right use of value.

Here are a handful of other guidelines that will add to your success in using color effectively.

There are no *absolutes* when it comes to using color—traditional color harmonies are good starting points for combining colors, but they are not meant to be rigid rules. Be creative and have fun as you play with various combinations of colors.

Color value is more important than color. Use the lightest tints and the deepest shades you can find of your favorite colors, and your quilts will become vibrant. If you love working in blues, think of the complete range of hues available, and use every blue, from pale, icy blue, to blue-violet, navy, blueberry, aquamarine, and the deepest other blue shades. Attempting to match all the blues in your quilt makes a dull and monotonous quilt. Using an unexpected blue will add excitement.

BUNKHOUSE SCRAPS
page 24

USING COLOR EFFECTIVELY

Make it a habit to emphasize one color or type of contrast in a quilt. Allow one color or mood to dominate the design, and let other colors and values enhance the dominant element. Remember that a small amount of a light color will balance a large amount of a darker color.

Don't try to *match* reds – red is **red**, so use a variety of textures and values in your chosen color.

Repeat an accent color in more than one place in a quilt. Use it in the quilt center, and/or echo it in the borders. The color complement of your dominant color makes a great accent color.

Consider the theme of your quilt when choosing a color combination. For example, red and black might not be a good color scheme for a wedding quilt, but it could be wonderful as a quilted banner in school colors.

Colors evoke certain moods and personalities. Think of some of the common phrases we use that illustrate this idea, including moody blues; sunny yellow; vivacious red; calm, green pastures; or cool, blue waters. You can use those colors to create the same moods in your quilts.

Color Value Tip

Take some time to look through your stash and sort your fabrics into piles according to values – light, medium, and dark. How many stacks of each value do you have? If you're like most quilters, you may find that many of your fabrics fall into the medium-value range. There are a couple of reasons for this. First, medium values feel "safe" to buy and use in a quilt. Second, there are more medium-value fabrics available on the market than darks and lights. Use this artist's value scale as a guide to sorting out the fabrics you now own. If you find yourself low in any particular area, make a point to visit your local quilt shop and scope out the latest offerings in those values.

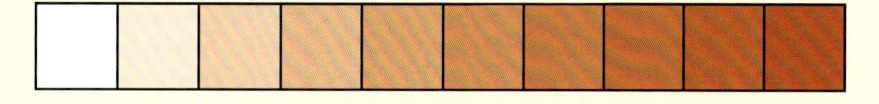

Nancy Brenan Daniel

Pretty Simple Quilts

Heirloom Quilts

Four-Patch & Nine-Patch

Finished blocks: 3" square
Finished quilt top: 40" x 52"

The colorful Nine-Patch and Four-Patch blocks in this FIELDS AND FURROWS setting add up to a striking baby or lap quilt. The small spots of warm yellow, gold, and rust fabrics in the Nine-Patch blocks are a nice contrast against the blue fabrics. This scrap quilt is very easy to enlarge or reduce to any size you desire.

Fabrics and Supplies

- ⅝ yard light solid fabric for Nine-Patch blocks
- ¾ yard light blue print fabric for Four-Patch blocks
- ¾ yard dark blue print fabric for Four-Patch blocks
- 1½ yards medium blue print fabric for Four-Patch blocks, border, and binding
- ⅛ yard each of 8 different fabrics in various warm colors, from dark yellow to rust
- 1¾ yards backing
- 44" x 56" piece of batting

Cutting Fabric

FOUR-PATCH BLOCKS A AND B

From the light blue print:
- Cut 4 – 3½" x 40" strips.

From the medium blue print:
- Cut 4 – 3½" x 40" strips.

From the dark blue print:
- Cut 4 – 3½" x 40" strips.

NINE-PATCH BLOCKS

From the light solid:
- Cut 10 – 1½" x 40" strips.

From the warm-colored:
- Cut 8 – 1½" x 40" strips.

BORDER AND BINDING

From the medium blue:
- Cut 5 – 2½" x 40" strips.
- Cut 5 – 2½" x 40" binding strips.

Piecing Four-Patch Block A

1. Sew a 3½" x 40" medium blue strip to a 3½" x 40" light blue strip. Press. Make 2 more strip-sets like this one. Sew a 3½" x 40" medium blue strip to a 3½" x 40" dark blue strip. Press. Make 2 more strip-sets like this one.

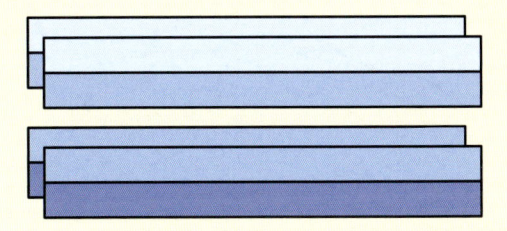

2. Cut the Step 1 strip-sets into 24 segments, each 3½" wide. Sew a segment from each set together to create Four-Patch Block A. Make 24 of Four-Patch block A.

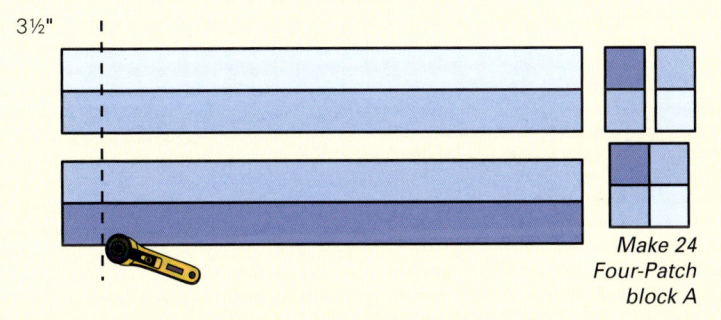

Make 24 Four-Patch block A

Piecing Four-Patch Block B

3. Sew a 1½" x 40" warm-colored strip to each side of a 1½" x 40" light solid strip. Press. Make a second strip-set like this one. Cut these strip-sets into 48 segments, each 1½" wide.

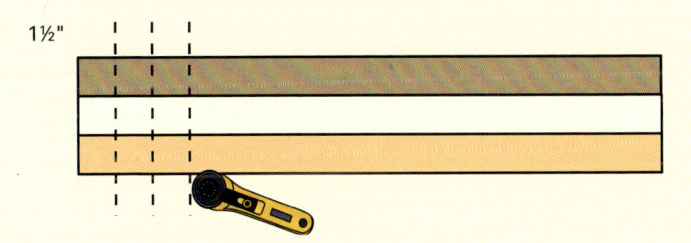

4. Sew 2 – 1½" x 40" light solid strips to each side of a 1½" x 40" warm-colored strip. Press. Make 3 more strip-sets like this one. Cut the 4 strip-sets into 96 segments, each 1½" wide.

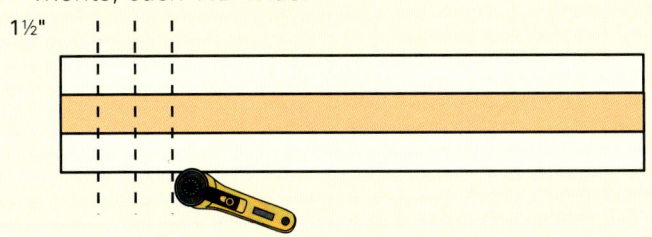

5. Sew a Step 4 segment to each side of a Step 3 segment to make a Nine-Patch block. Press. Make 48 Nine-Patch blocks.

Make 48 Nine-Patch Blocks

6. Sew 24 Nine-Patch blocks to the 3 – 3½" x 40" light blue strips. Cut the light blue fabric even with the edges of the Nine-Patch blocks. Press the seam allowances toward the light blue fabric.

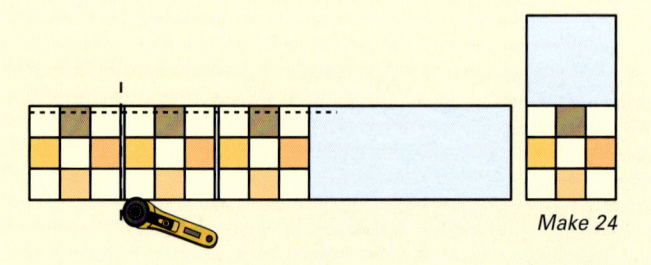

Make 24

7. Sew 24 Nine-Patch blocks to 3 – 3½" x 40" dark blue strips. Cut the dark blue fabric even with the edges of the Nine-Patch blocks. Press the seam allowances toward the dark blue fabric.

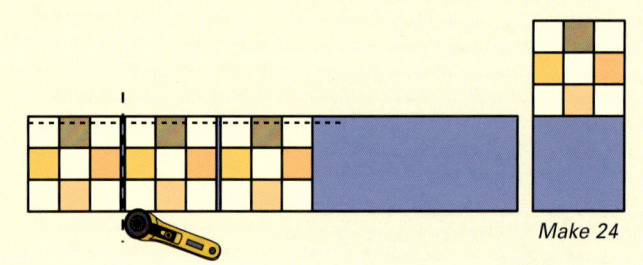

Make 24

8. Sew a Step 6 segment to a Step 7 segment to create Four-Patch block B. Make 24 of Four-Patch block B.

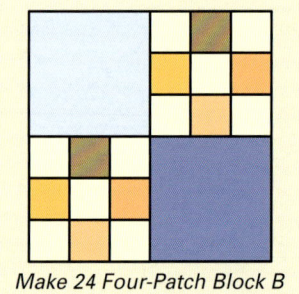

Make 24 Four-Patch Block B

Assembling the Quilt Center

9. Sew the blocks together in 10 rows of 6 blocks each, alternating the placement of Four-Patch blocks A and B. Press the seam allowances in each row in opposite directions.

10. Referring to the previous illustration, sew the rows of blocks together, completing the quilt center. Press.

Adding the Border

11. Measure your quilt from side to side through the middle to determine the correct length for the top and bottom border strips. Trim 2 – 2½" x 40" medium blue border strips to this measurement and sew them to the top and bottom edges of the quilt center, referring to the previous diagram. Press the seam allowances toward the border strips.

12. Measure your quilt top vertically through the middle, including the borders you just added, to determine the correct length for the side border strips. Sew the remaining 2½" x 40" border strips together, press these seam allowances open, and cut 2 border strips to the correct measurement. Sew these border strips to the sides of the quilt center, referring to the previous diagram. Press the seam allowances toward the border strips.

Finishing

13. Place the quilt backing wrong side up on a flat surface. Add the batting and the completed quilt top. Baste the 3 layers together.

14. Quilt as desired, by hand or machine.

15. Apply the binding to the edges of the quilt.

FOUR-PATCH & NINE-PATCH

QUILT ASSEMBLY

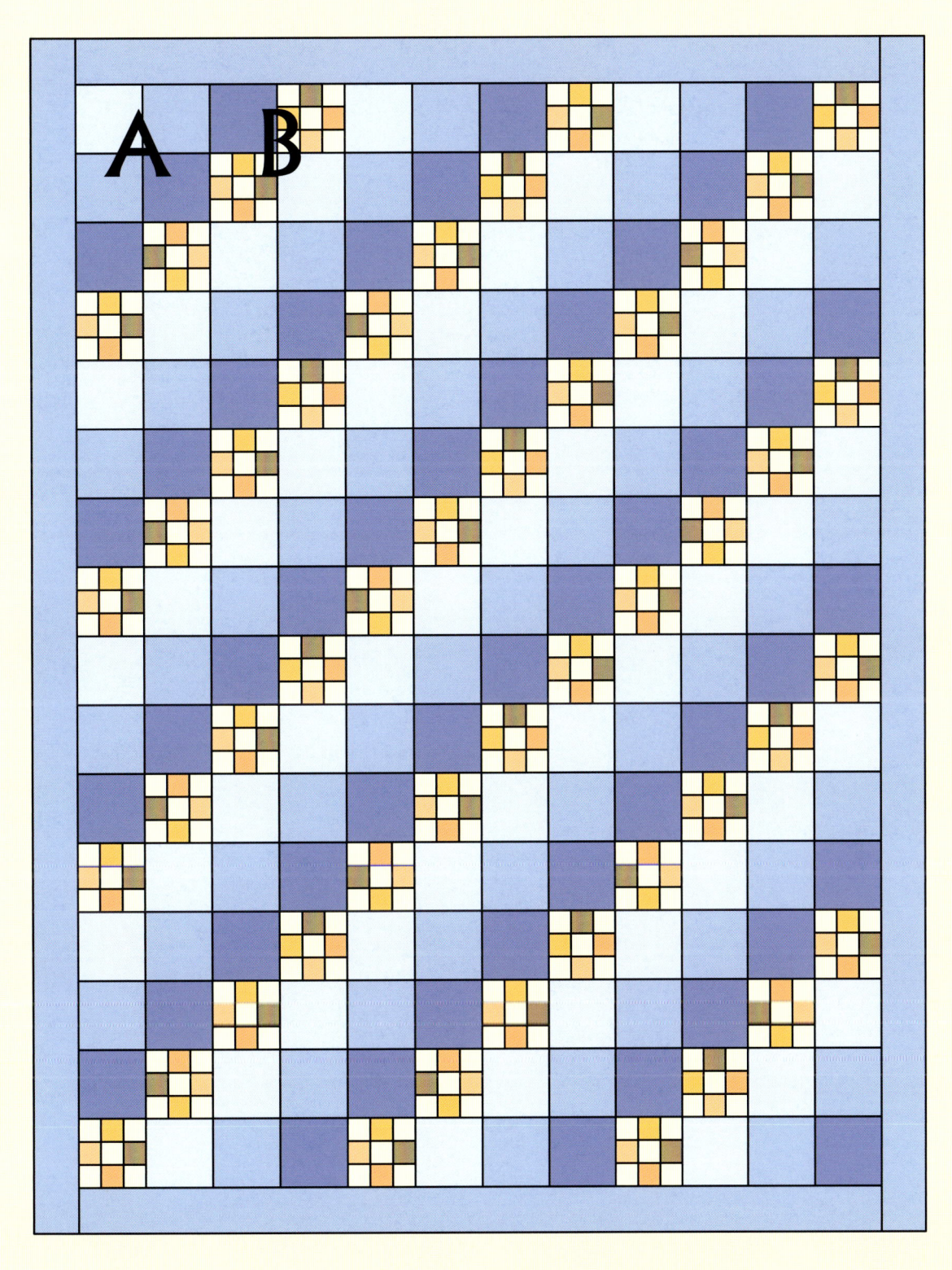

Quilt assembly

Nancy Brenan Daniel — 13 — Pretty Simple Quilts

Stars & Spinners

Finished blocks: 6" square
Finished quilt top: 48½" x 60½"

The red and blue "spinners" at the ends of the stars may put your mind in a dizzy whirl. This pattern is actually easy to make, using 2 simple blocks for the center of the quilt and half blocks to complete the spinners at the edges of the quilt.

Pretty Simple Quilts   Nancy Brenan Daniel

Fabrics and Supplies

- 2 yards medium blue fabric for background
- ¼ yard each of three different blue print fabrics for stars
- 1 yard red solid fabric for spinners and inner border
- 2 yards dark blue print fabric for spinners, outer border, and binding
- 3 yards of fabric for backing (or 2 yards of 60"-wide fabric)

Cutting Fabric

BLOCK A

From each of the three light blues:
- Cut three 2" x width of fabric strips.

From the medium blue background:
- Cut 7 – 2" x width of fabric strips.

From the dark blue print:
- Cut 4 – 2" x width of fabric strips. From these strips, cut 72 squares, each 2" x 2".

From the red solid:
- Cut 4 – 2" x width of fabric strips. From these strips, cut 72 squares, each 2" x 2".

BLOCK B

From the medium blue background:
- Cut 7 – 3½" x width of fabric strips. From these strips, cut 68 squares, each 3½" x 3½".

From the dark blue print:
- Cut 4 – 2" x width of fabric strips. From these strips, cut 68 squares, each 2" x 2".

From the red solid:
- Cut 4 – 2" x width of fabric strips. From these strips, cut 68 squares, each 2" x 2".

HALF AND CORNER BLOCKS

From the medium blue background:
- Cut 5 – 3½" x width of fabric strips. From these strips, cut 52 squares, each 3½" x 3½".

From the dark blue print:
- Cut 2 – 2" x width of fabric strips. From these strips, cut 24 squares, each 2" x 2".

From the red solid:
- Cut 2 – 2" x width of fabric strips. From these strips, cut 24 squares, each 2" x 2".

INNER BORDER
From the red solid:
- Cut 5 strips, each 2" x width of fabric.

OUTER BORDER AND BINDING
From the dark blue print:
- Cut 6 strips, each 5¼" x width of fabric.
- Cut 6 strips, each 2½" x width of fabric.

Piecing Block A

1. Sew a light blue print strip to a medium blue background strip and press. Repeat for the remaining light blue print and medium blue background strips. Cut 72 – 3½" squares from these strip-sets.

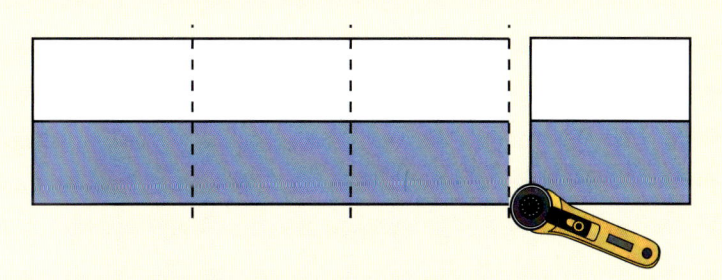

2. Place a 2" red square on one corner of the Step 1 unit, and a dark blue square at the opposite corner. Sew diagonally across these squares, as shown. Flip the triangles over and trim the excess fabric on the wrong side to a ¼" seam allowance at each corner. Press. Make a total of 72 of these units, taking care to be consistent each time you sew the 2" squares in place.

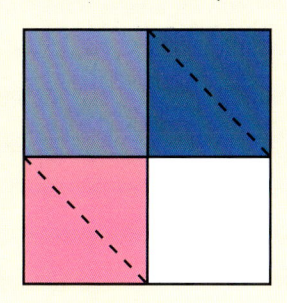

Make 72

3. Sew 4 Step 2 units together to complete Block A. Make 18 of Block A.

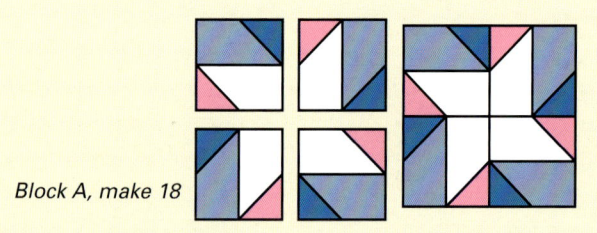

Block A, make 18

Piecing Block B

4. In the same manner, sew a 2" red square and a 2" dark blue square at opposite corners of a 3½" medium blue background square. Press and trim the excess fabric to ¼". Make 68 of these units.

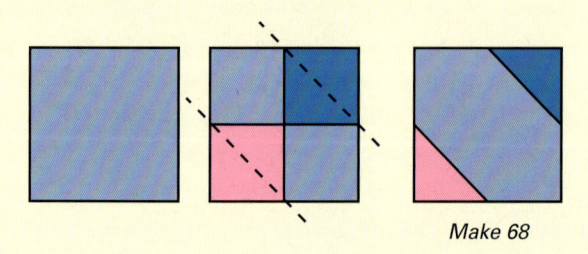

Make 68

5. Sew 4 Step 4 units together to complete Block B. Make 17 of Block B.

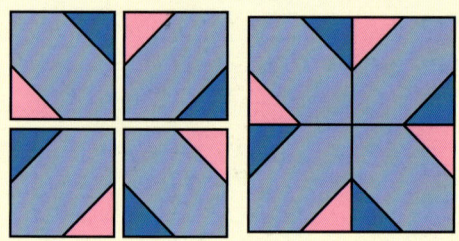

Block B, make 17

Piecing the Half Blocks

6. Sew a 2" red square to a 3½" medium blue background square and press. Sew a 2" dark blue square to a medium blue background square. Press and trim as before.

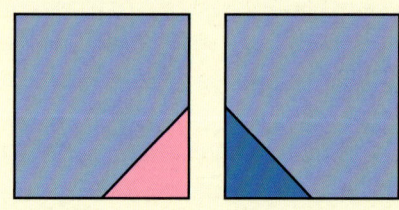

7. Sew the 2 Step 6 units together to complete a half-block. Make 24 Half blocks.

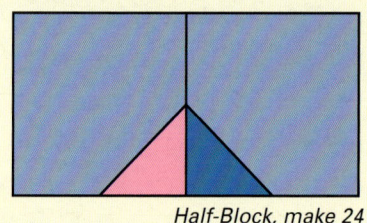

Half-Block, make 24

Assembling the Quilt Center

8. Sew 3 Block A and 2 Block B together, as shown and press. Make 4 of these rows.

Make 4 rows

9. Sew 3 Block B and 2 Block A together, as shown, and press. Make 3 of these rows.

Make 3 rows

10. Sew the 7 rows together, alternating them, as shown below. Press.

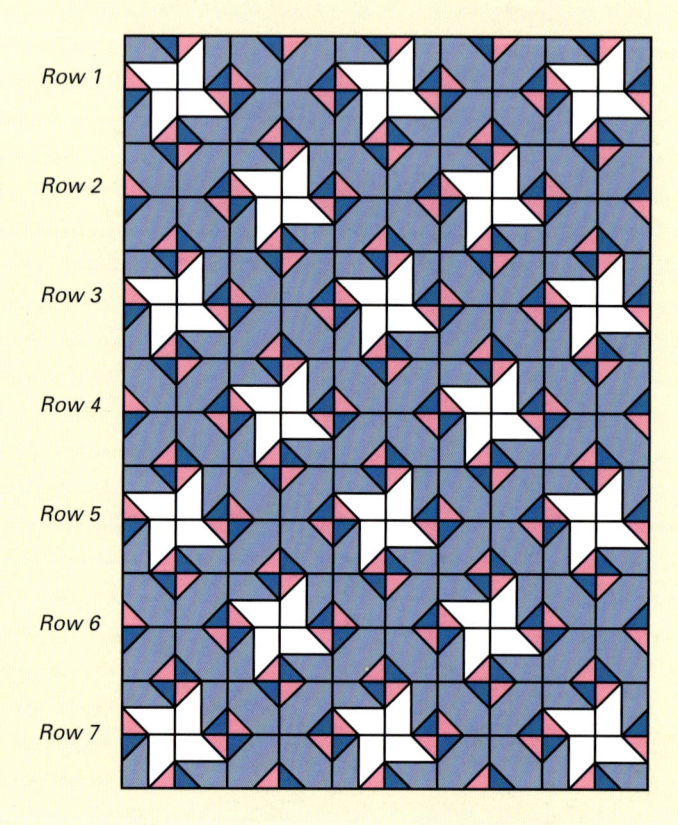

Row 1
Row 2
Row 3
Row 4
Row 5
Row 6
Row 7

Adding Corner and Half Blocks

11. Make 2 rows of 5 half blocks and press. Referring to the Quilt Assembly diagram, page 21, sew them to the top and bottom edges of the quilt and press.

12. Make 2 rows of 7 half blocks, adding a plain 3½" square at each end, and press. Sew them to the sides of the quilt and press.

Pretty Simple Quilts — Nancy Brenan Daniel

STARS & SPINNERS

QUILT ASSEMBLY

13. Add the 2" red solid inner border strips to the quilt. Press.

14. Add the 5¼" dark blue outer border strips to the quilt. Press.

Finishing

15. Place the quilt backing wrong side up on a flat surface. Add the batting and the completed quilt top. Baste the 3 layers together.

16. Quilt as desired, by hand or machine.

17. Apply the binding to the edges of the quilt.

MARCH PINWHEELS

Finished panels: 12" x 48"
Finished quilt top: 48" x 60"

A single sunflower was the inspiration for this gathering of flowers and pinwheels.

Fabric and Supplies

- 2¼ yards light blue variegated for background
- ¾ yard assorted dark blue prints for the Pinwheel blocks
- ¾ yard assorted red prints for the flowers and buds
- 1 yard of one red print for the outer border and binding
- ½ yard assorted green prints for the stems and leaves
- ⅛ yard black print for the flower centers
- ⅛ yard gold print for the flower centers
- 3 yards backing (or 1⅞ yards of 60"-wide fabric)
- 52" x 64" piece of batting

Cutting Fabric

FLOWER AND BUD BLOCKS

From the light blue variegated:
- Cut 5 strips, each 2½" x 40". From these strips, cut 66 squares, each 2½" x 2½".
- Cut 3 strips, each 2½" x 40". From these strips, cut 18 rectangles, each 2½" x 4½".
- Cut the remaining background fabric using the measurements in the layout diagrams (pages 21–22).

From the assorted red prints:
- Cut 2 strips, each 2½" x 40". From these strips, cut 19 squares, each 2½" x 2½".
- Cut 3 strips, each 2½" x 40". From these strips, cut 18 rectangles, each 2½" x 4½".
- Cut 3 strips, each 2½" x 40". From these strips, cut 18 rectangles, each 2½" x 6½".

From the assorted green prints:
- Cut 3 strips, each 1½" x 40". From these strips, cut 6 rectangles, each 1½" x 6½"; 2 rectangles, each 1½" x 18½"; a 1½" x 8½" rectangle; and a 1½" x 16½" rectangle.
- Cut a 2½" x 40" strip. From this strip, cut 9 squares, each 2½" x 2½".
- Cut a 2½" x 40" strip. From this strip cut 7 rectangles 2½" x 4½"; 1 rectangle 2½" x 6½".

From the black print:
- Cut a 4" x 40" strip. From this strip, cut 6 squares, each 4" x 4".

From the gold print:
- Cut a 4" x 40" strip. From this strip, cut 6 squares, each 4" x 4".

PINWHEEL BORDER AND PINWHEEL BLOCKS

You need 204 half-square triangle units to make 51 Pinwheel Blocks—5 for the quilt top and 46 for the border. Cut triangles as indicted below OR save the yardage for your own favorite method of making half-square triangles.

From the light blue variegated prints:
- Cut 8 strips, each 2⅞" x 40". From these strips, cut 102 squares, each 2⅞" x 2⅞". Cut these squares in half diagonally for a total of 204 triangles.

From the dark blue prints:
- Cut 8 strips, each 2⅞"" x 40". From these strips, cut 102 squares, each 2⅞"" x 2⅞". Cut these squares in half diagonally for a total of 204 triangles.

BORDER AND BINDING

From the red print:
- Cut 6 strips, each 2½" x 40".
- Cut 6 – 2½" x 40" binding strips.

Piecing the Flower, Bud, and Pinwheel Blocks

1. Sew 19 red print 2½" x 2½" squares to 19 blue variegated 2½" x 2½" squares. Press.

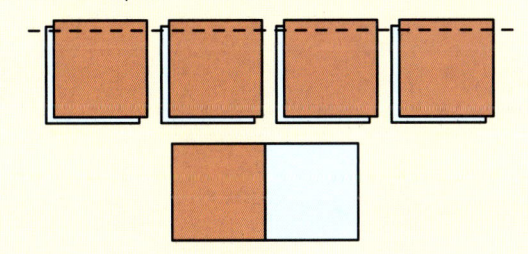

2. Sew a blue variegated 2½" x 4½" rectangle to 13 of the Step 1 units. Press. Reserve the 6 remaining Step 1 units.

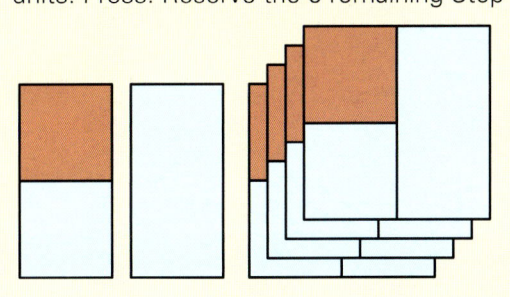

3. Sew 2 blue variegated 2½" x 2½" squares to the ends of 6 green print 2½" x 4½" rectangles with diagonal seams, as shown. These leaf units must be mirror images of each other.

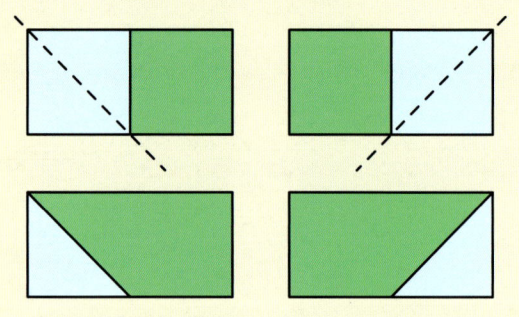

In the same manner, sew 2 blue variegated 2½" x 2½" squares to the opposite ends of the green rectangles. Press and trim the excess fabric on the wrong side to a ¼" seam allowance.

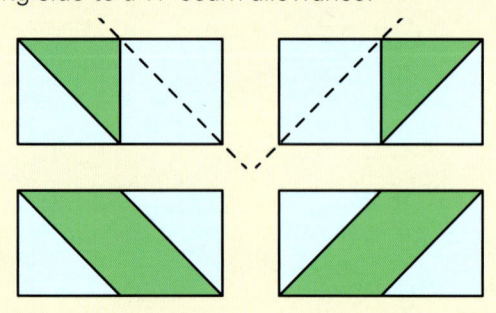

4. Sew the 6 Step 3 leaf units to the reserved Step 2 units, as shown.

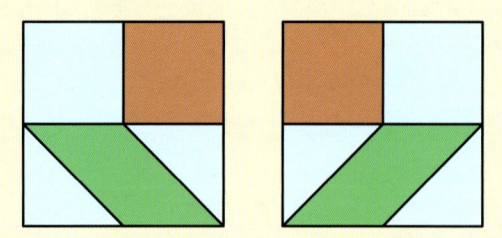

5. Add 2½" x 4½" and 2½" x 6½" red rectangles to the 6 leaf units and 12 of the Step 2 units as shown. Add 2½" x 4½" and 2½" x 6½" green rectangles to the remining Step 2 unit (this will become the bud in Panel A).

6. With diagonal seams, sew a green 2½" x 2½" square to 3 of the leaf units and a blue variegated 2½" x 2½" square to the remaining 3 leaf units. Press and trim the excess fabric as before.

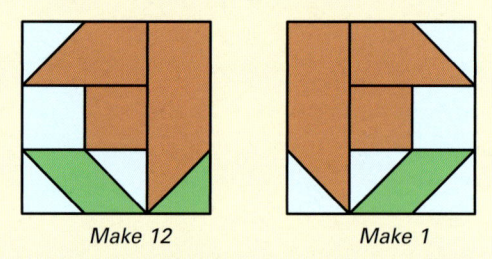

Make 12   Make 1

7. Sew 2 blue variegated 2½" x 2½" squares to opposite corners of 12 Step 5 units. Sew 2½" x 2½" squares to 3 corners of the remaining Step 5 unit (the bud).

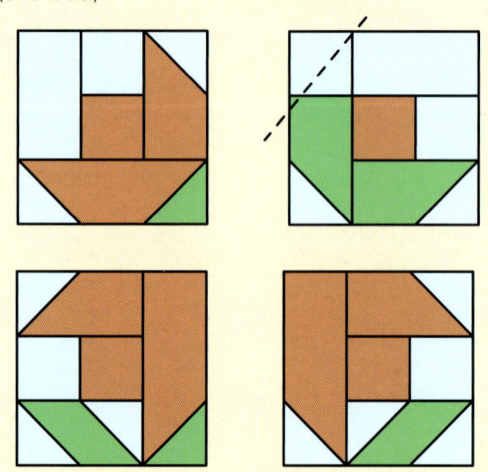

8. With a diagonal seam, sew a gold 4" x 4" square to the corner of 3 leaf units and 3 of the 12 Step 7 units. In the same way, sew a black 4" x 4" square to the corner to the remaining leaf units and 3 of the Step 7 units.

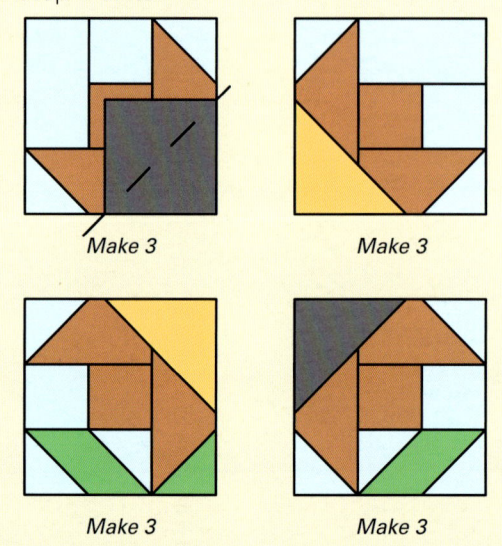

Make 3   Make 3

Make 3   Make 3

9. Use the blue variegated and dark blue print triangles or your favorite method to make 204 –2½" x 2½" half-square triangle units.

Pretty Simple Quilts — - 20 - — Nancy Brenan Daniel

Four-Patch & Nine-Patch | Quilt Assembly

10. Sew the Step 9 half-square triangle units together in pairs. Press. Sew each of the 4 pairs of half-square triangle units together to complete 2 Pinwheel blocks. Press.

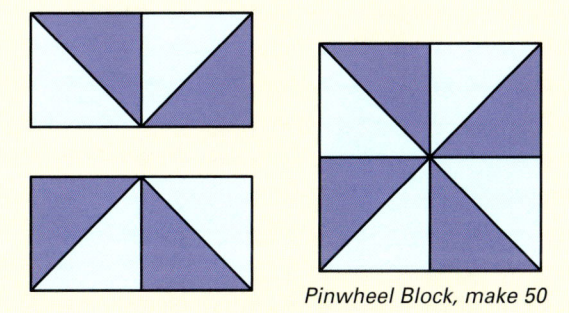

Pinwheel Block, make 50

Assembling Panels A, B & C

Refer to the individual panel diagrams (see page 22 for Panel B and Panel C) for pieced units, cut sizes, and assembly. Sew the panels into horizontal sections, then sew the sections together and press.

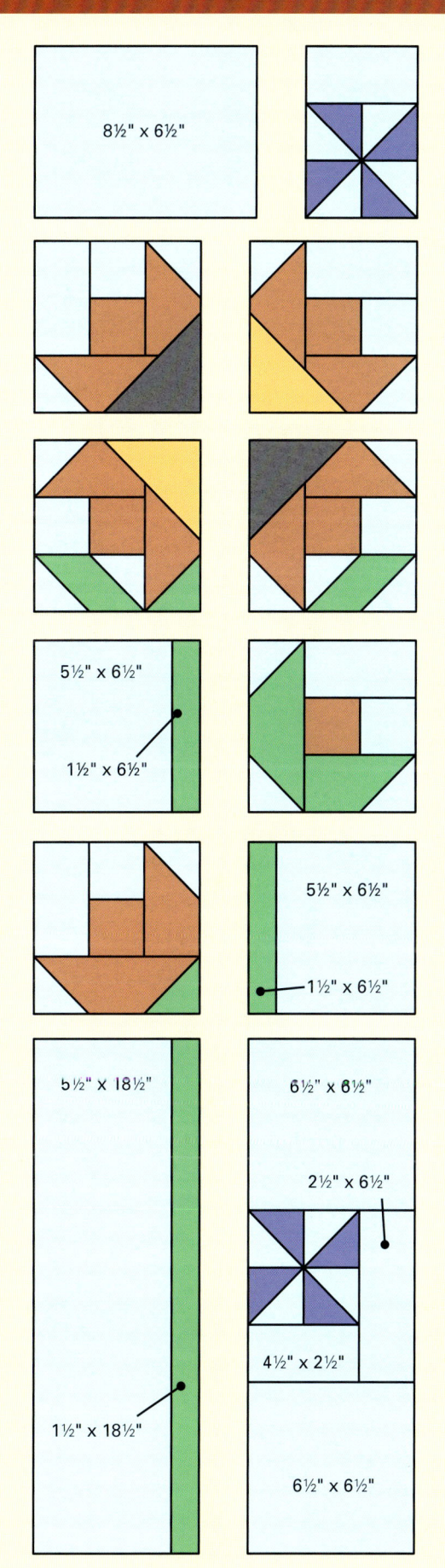

8½" x 6½"

5½" x 6½"
1½" x 6½"

5½" x 6½"
1½" x 6½"

5½" x 18½"
1½" x 18½"

6½" x 6½"
2½" x 6½"
4½" x 2½"
6½" x 6½"

Nancy Brenan Daniel — 21 — Pretty Simple Quilts

PANEL B

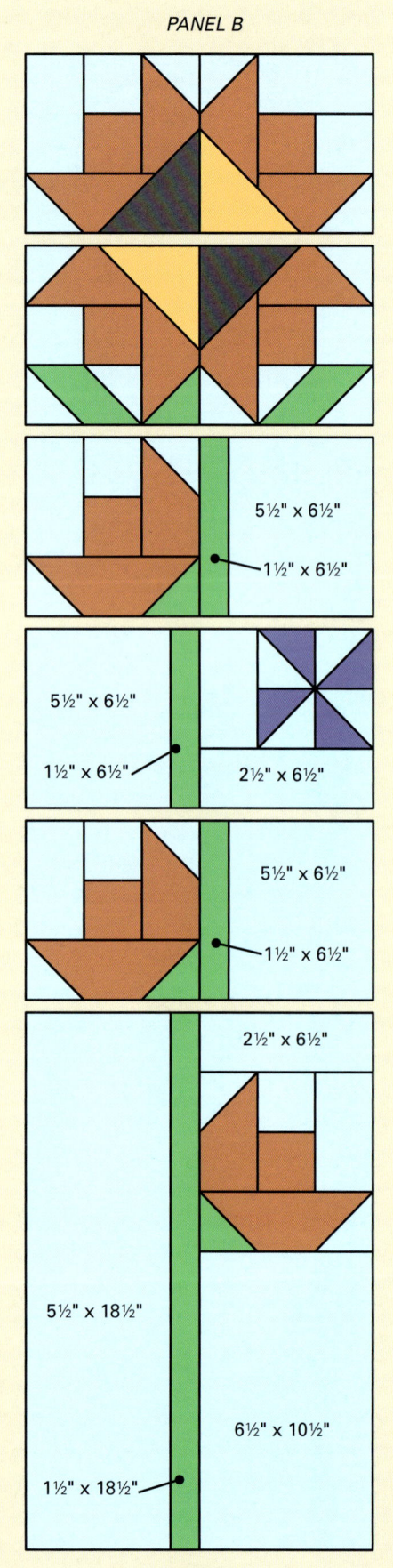

PANEL C

2½" x 4½"
6½" x 6½"
2½" x 6½"

5½" x 6½"
1½" x 6½"

5½" x 6½"
1½" x 6½"
2½" x 6½"

5½" x 8½"
2½" x 6½"
1½" x 8½"

5½" x 6½"
1½" x 6½"

5½" x 6½"
1½" x 6½"

2½" x 6½"

6½" x 12½"
5½" x 16½"
1½" x 16½"

5½" x 18½"
6½" x 10½"
1½" x 18½"

There are small variations in the number and placement of the Bud blocks and Pinwheel blocks in Panel B.

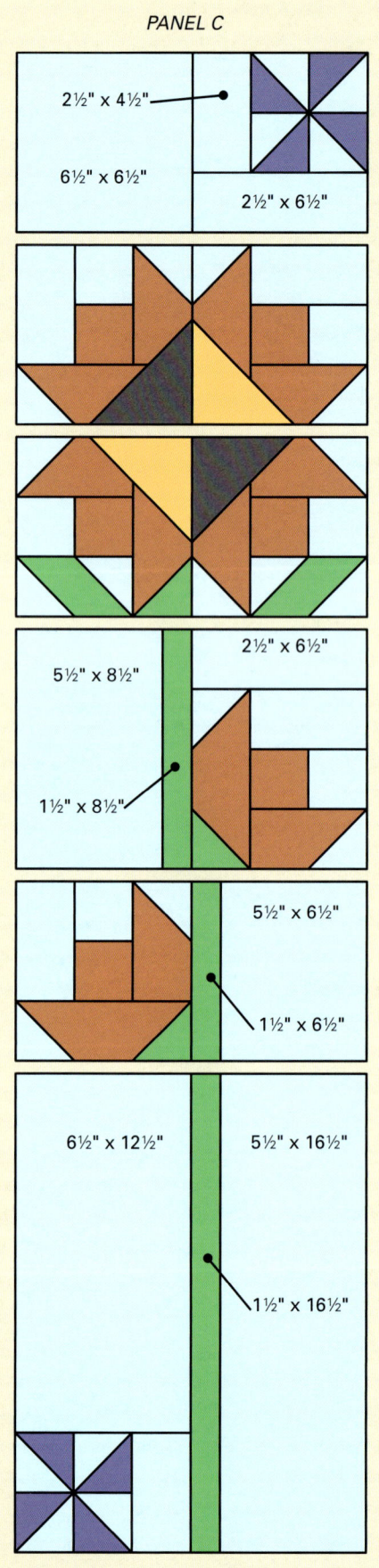

Note that the Pinwheel block in the upper right corner faces the opposite direction from other Pinwheel blocks in the quilt.

Pretty Simple Quilts — 22 — Nancy Brenan Daniel

MARCH PINWHEELS   QUILT ASSEMBLY

Adding the Pinwheel Border

11. Sew two sets of 9 Pinwheel blocks together and sew to the top and bottom. Press. Sew 14 Pinwheel blocks together for each side border. Add to the sides of the quilt. Press.

Adding the Outer Border

12. Measure your quilt top to determine the correct measurement for the top and bottom outer border strips. Trim 2 – 2½"-wide red print strips to this length and sew them to the top and bottom edges of the quilt. Press the seam allowances toward the borders. Piece the remaining red print 2½" x 40" strips together in pairs. Press the seam allowances open. Measure your quilt top vertically through the middle to determine the correct measurement for the side outer border strips. Trim the pieced strips to this length and sew them to the sides of the quilt. Press the seam allowances toward the borders.

Finishing

13. Place the quilt backing wrong side up on a flat surface. Add the batting and the completed quilt top. Baste the 3 layers together.

14. Quilt as desired, by hand or machine.

15. Apply the binding to the edges of the quilt.

Nancy Brenan Daniel   Pretty Simple Quilts

BUNKHOUSE SCRAPS

Finished Feathered Patchwork strip width: 1½"
Finished quilt top: 86" x 110"

Antique woven rugs, similar to BUNKHOUSE SCRAPS, are called "eye-dazzlers" or "Germantown" after the bright worsted wool from which they were made in the early American West. This quilt reflects the same grand tradition in the form of a quilt. Its reproduction-style prints and colors are reminiscent of the turn of the nineteenth century.

Bunkhouse Scraps

Fabrics and Supplies
- 3 yards assorted light and medium prints for Feathered Patchwork strips
- 4¼ yards assorted dark print for Feathered Patchwork strips
- 2¼ yards of one medium blue print for end wedges, side strips, and triangles
- ½ yard of light print for pieced border
- 1¼ yard assorted bright and dark prints for pieced border
- 2⅝ yards of one dark blue print for outer border and binding
- 7¾ yards backing (or 3¼ yards of 90"-wide fabric)
- 90" x 114" piece of batting

Cutting Fabrics

Feathered Patchwork Strips
From the light and medium prints:
- Cut 17 strips, each 6" x 40". From these strips, cut 84 triangles.

From the assorted dark prints:
- Cut 23 strips, each 6" x 40". From these strips, cut 112 triangles.

From the medium blue print:
- Cut 3 strips, each 6" x 40". From these strips, cut 14 triangles.
- Cut 6 strips, each 6" x 40". From these strips, cut 14 pairs of end wedges.

Pieced Border
From the light prints:
- Cut 8 strips 2⅝" x 40". From these cut 112 –2⅝" x 2⅝" squares.

From the bright and dark prints:
- Cut 16 strips, each 2¾" x 40". From these strips, cut 224 squares, each 2¾" x 2¾". Cut these squares in half diagonally for a total of 448 triangles.

Outer Border and Binding
From the dark blue print:
- Cut 10 strips, each 6" x 40".
- Cut 11 2½" x 40" binding strips.

Cutting the End Wedges and Triangles

1. Fold the medium blue print strips in half and use the following dimensions to cut the 14 pairs of end wedges. Cut 2 end wedges at a time on each folded strip, and open up the fabric to cut one more end wedge from each strip, right side up. Be sure to alternate the angle each time you cut a single end wedge.

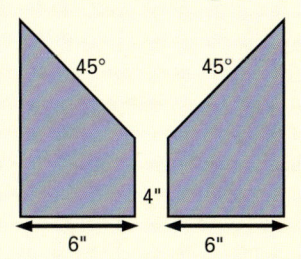

2. To cut the triangles from the assorted light, medium, and dark prints, place a 6" x 24" acrylic ruler on the strip, aligning the 45° angle line with the edge of the strip. Make the first cut. Then rotate the ruler and repeat the process to cut the other side of the triangle. Take care to cut each triangle accurately.

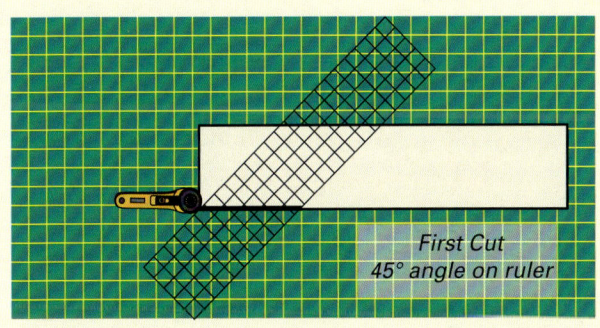

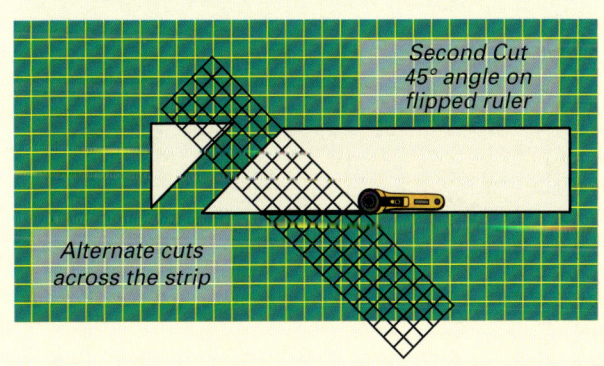

3. To ensure piecing accuracy, use a pencil to mark the center of every light, medium, and dark triangle so it will be easy to align the triangles correctly as you piece each Feathered Patchwork strip.

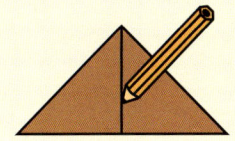

Piecing Feathered Patchwork Strips
Make 14 Feathered Patchwork strips, each consisting

Nancy Brenan Daniel — Pretty Simple Quilts

of 8 dark triangles, 7 light or medium triangles, and a pair of end wedges. It is helpful to try out the piecing technique with scrap fabrics before piecing your Feathered Patchwork strips.

4. Sew a dark triangle to an end wedge, offsetting the center mark on the triangle ¼" from the long edge of the wedge and aligning the angled edges. Press the seam allowance toward the darker fabric throughout.

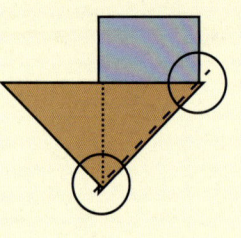

5. Continue adding triangles to the Feathered Patchwork Strip, alternating the dark triangles with the light or medium triangles and offsetting the center mark ¼" from the long straight edge of the strip as before. Add the end wedge after the eighth dark triangle. There will be a ¼" seam allowance at the tip of each triangle.

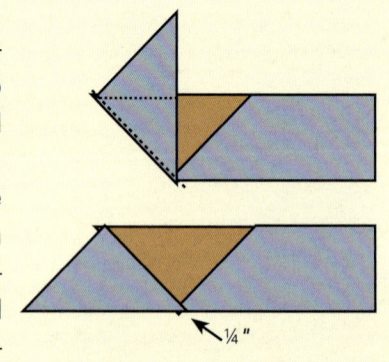

6. Lay out the 14 Feathered Patchwork strips as shown below. Sew 2 – 3½" wide medium blue print strips end to end and lay to the left of the Feathered Patchwork strip #1. Repeat and lay the second strip to the right of strip #14.

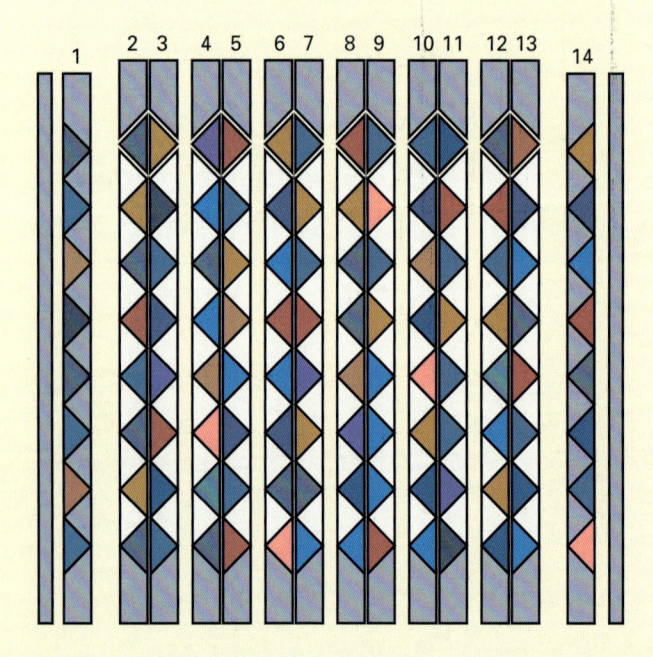

7. One at a time, carefully cut each Feathered Patchwork strip into 3 – 2" wide segments. Rearrange the segments as shown and sew them together again. Press the seam allowances open.

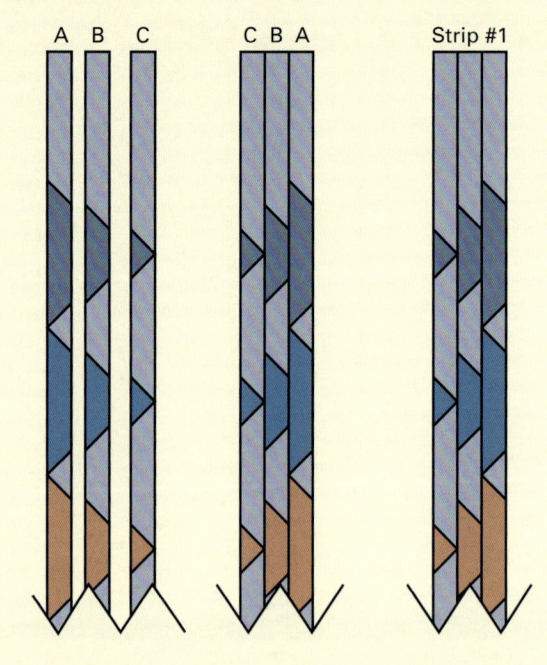

8. Add the medium blue strips to re-pieced Strip #1 and Strip #14. Join the remaining strips into pairs (#2 & #3, #4 & #5, and so on). Then join all the units to finish the center of the quilt top. Press the seam allowances open.

9. Trim the top and bottom edges of the quilt center so that it measures 93½" long.

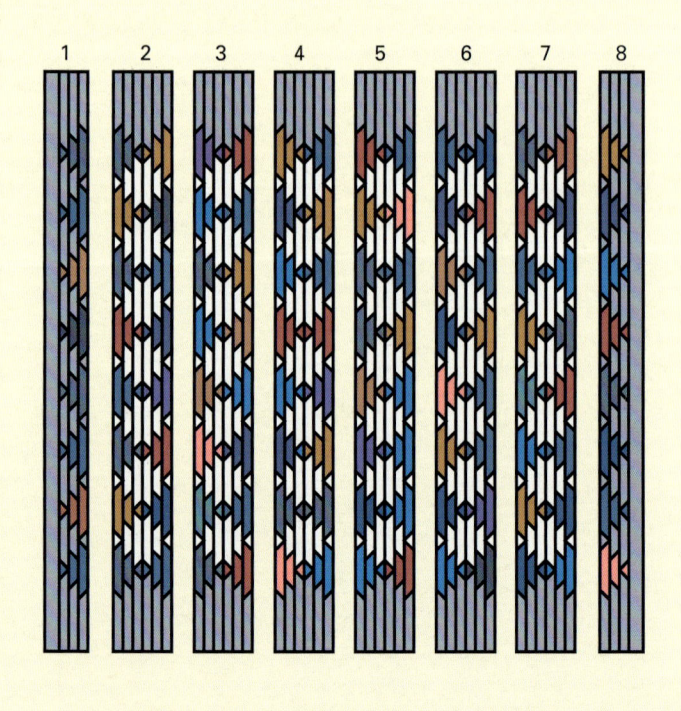

Pretty Simple Quilts — Nancy Brenan Daniel

Adding the Pieced Border

10. Sew 4 bright or dark triangles to each 2⅜" light square. Make a total of 112 of these units.

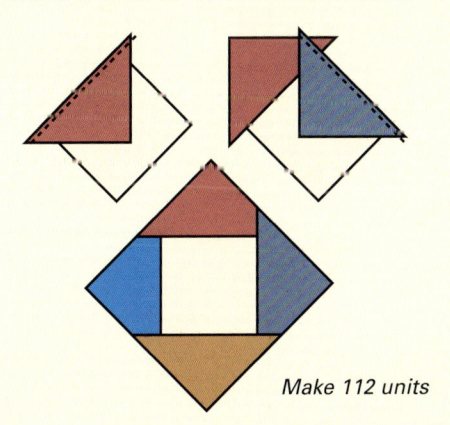

Make 112 units

11. Sew 31 Step 10 units together for each side of the quilt. Press the seam allowances open and sew these pieced units to the sides of the quilt center. Sew 25 Step 10 units together for the top and bottom edges of the quilt center and press the seam allowances open. Sew these pieced units to the top and bottom edges of the quilt. Refer to the Quilt Assembly diagram above.

Adding the Outer Border

12. Sew remaining 40" dark blue print border strips together and press the seam allowance open. Repeat to make another border strip like this one. Measure your quilt to determine the correct length for the top, bottom, and side border strips. Cut the pieced strips to these lengths and sew them to the quilt, referring to the diagram above. Press the seam allowances toward the borders.

Finishing

13. Place the quilt backing wrong side up on a flat surface. Add the batting and the completed quilt top. Baste the 3 layers together.

14. Quilt as desired, by hand or machine.

15. Apply the binding to the edges of the quilt.

Almost Amish

Finished blocks: 6" square
Finished quilt top: 40" x 40"

Many Amish-style quilts are boldly graphic. They are the result of a very straightforward way of dealing with value and color contrast. Many modern quiltmakers and collectors are drawn to the contemporary look and calm elegance of older Amish quilts. The title of this quilt comes from the use of colors that would not likely be found in a traditional Amish quilt.

Fabrics and Supplies

- 1⅞ yards solid black
- 1 yard of scraps in assorted bright colors
- 1½ yards backing
- 44" x 44" piece of batting

Cutting Fabrics

Gretchen Blocks

From the solid black:

- Cut a 4⅞" x 40" strip. From this strip, cut 8 – 4⅞" x 4⅞" squares. Cut these squares in half diagonally.
- Cut 2 – 2⅞" x 40" strips. From these strips, cut 16 – 2⅞" x 2⅞" squares. Cut these squares in half diagonally.
- Cut 4 – 2" x 40" strips. From these strips, cut 16 – 2" x 6⅞" rectangles.

From the brights:

- Cut 8 – 4⅞" x 4⅞," squares. Cut these squares in half diagonally.
- Cut 16 – 2⅞" x 2⅞" squares. Cut these squares in half diagonally.
- Cut 16 – 2" x 6⅞" rectangles.

Inner Sawtooth Border

From the solid black:

- Cut 2 – 2⅞" x 40" strips. From these strips, cut 24 – 2⅞" x 2⅞" squares. Cut these squares in half diagonally.
- Cut 4 – 2½" x 2½" squares.

From the brights:

- Cut 4 – 4½" x 40" strips.

Outer Sawtooth Border and Binding

From the black solid:

- Cut 3 – 2⅞" x 40" strips. From these strips, cut 36 – 2⅞" x 2⅞" squares. Cut these squares in half diagonally.
- Cut 4 – 2½" x 2½" squares.
- Cut 5 – 2½" x 40" binding strips.

From the brights:

- Cut 36 – 2⅞" x 2⅞" squares. Cut these squares in half diagonally.

Piecing the Gretchen Blocks

1. With right sides together, chain-piece the 16 large bright triangles to the 16 – 2" x 6⅞" black rectangles. In the same manner, chain piece the 16 large black triangles to the 16 – 2" x 6⅞" bright rectangles. Cut the threads between these units and press the seam allowances toward the darker fabric.

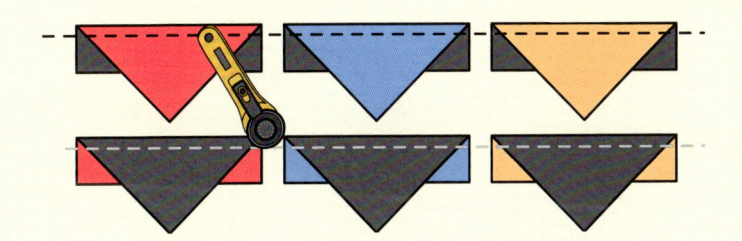

2. Align 2 small bright triangles with each Step 1 unit featuring a black rectangle. The edges of the small bright triangles should be even with the edges of the large bright triangle. Repeat this step, using 2 small black triangles and the second group of Step 1 units.

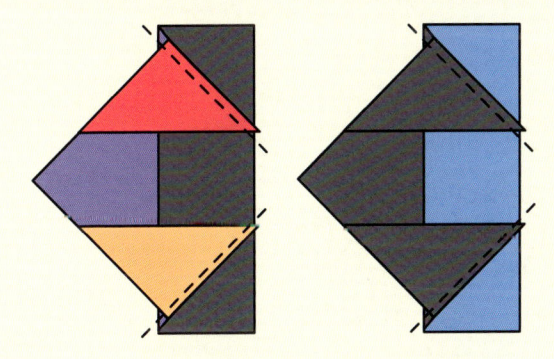

3. Trim the excess fabric from the rectangles and press the seam allowances of the small triangles toward the darker fabric. You should have 32 half block units.

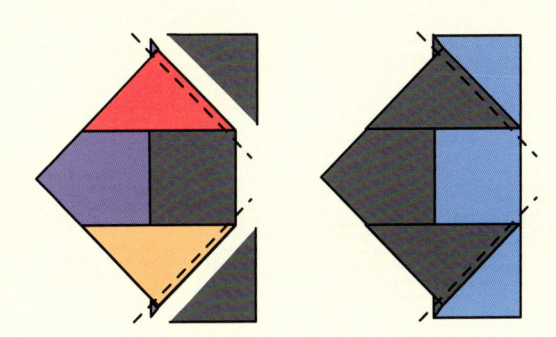

Nancy Brenan Daniel — Pretty Simple Quilts

4. Place the 2 halves of each Gretchen block side by side; one unit with a large bright triangle and one with a large darker triangle.

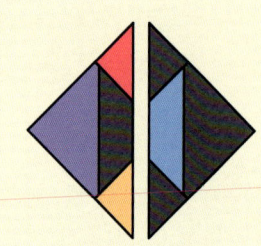

5. Pin the units together where the smaller triangles meet at the ¼" seam allowance and sew the 2 units together. Open the 2 units and press the center seam open. Make 16 Gretchen blocks.

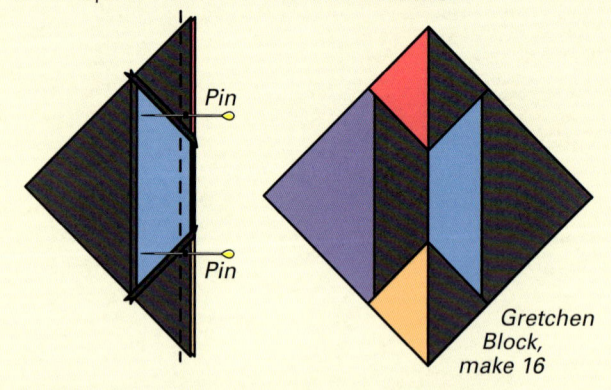

Gretchen Block, make 16

Assembling the Quilt Center

6. Sew 4 horizontal rows of 4 blocks each, alternating the diagonal seams of each block. Press.

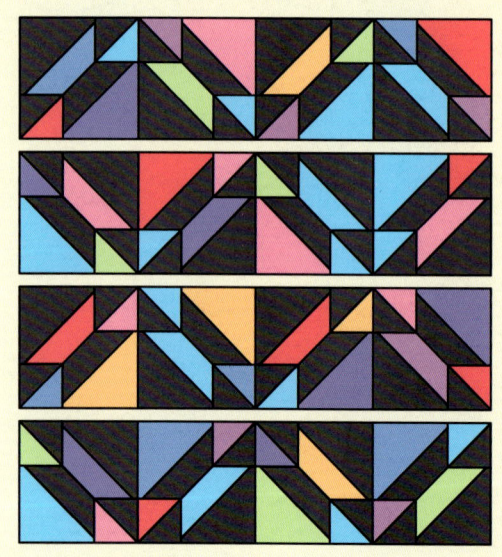

7. Sew the 4 rows together to complete the quilt center. Press.

Adding the Inner Sawtooth Border

Note: You need a total of 116 half-square triangle units for the 2 Sawtooth borders.

8. Sew 48 half-square triangle units, using the black and bright triangles. Press. Sew 4 strips of 12 half-square triangle units each. Press. Sew a 2½" black square at each end of 2 of these strips. Press. With the brights toward the center, sew the 2 strips with 12 half-square triangle units to the top and bottom edges of the quilt center.

9. Sew the 2 strips with black squares to the sides of the quilt center, with the brights toward the Gretchen blocks.

Adding the Middle Border

10. Measure your quilt top from side to side through the middle to determine the correct length for the top and bottom border strips. Trim 2 – 4½" x 40" black strips to this measurement and sew them to the top and bottom edges of the quilt. Press.

Pretty Simple Quilts — Nancy Brenan Daniel

11. Measure your quilt top vertically through the middle, including the border strips you just added. Trim 2 – 4½" x 40" black border strips to this measurement. Referring to the diagram above, sew them to the sides of the quilt. Press.

Adding the Outer Sawtooth Border

12. Referring to Step 8, sew 68 half-square triangle units, using the black and bright triangles.

13. Referring to the diagram above, sew 4 strips of 18 half-square triangle units each. Press. Sew a 2½" black square at each end of 2 of these strips. Press. With the brights toward the outside, sew the 2 strips with 18 half-square triangle units to the top and bottom edges of the quilt. Press. Sew the 2 strips with black squares to the sides of the quilt. Press.

Finishing

14. Place the quilt backing wrong side up on a flat surface. Add the batting and the completed quilt top. Baste the 3 layers together.

15. Quilt as desired, by hand or machine.

16. Apply the binding to the edges of the quilt.

More Love to Quilt Books

This is only a small selection of books available from Love to Quilt. Look for them at your local bookseller, fabric store, quilt shop, or public library.

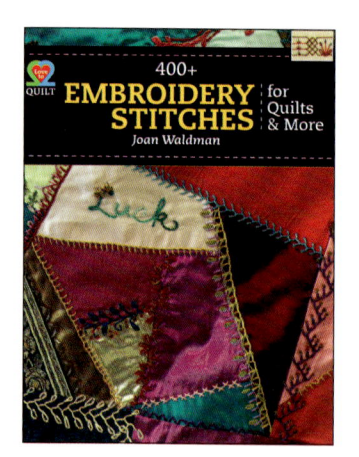

400+ Embroidery Stitches for Quilts & More — Joan Waldman #1274 .... $12.95	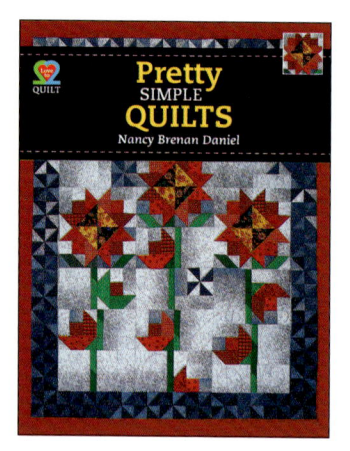 Pretty Simple Quilts — Nancy Brenan Daniel #1278 .... $12.95	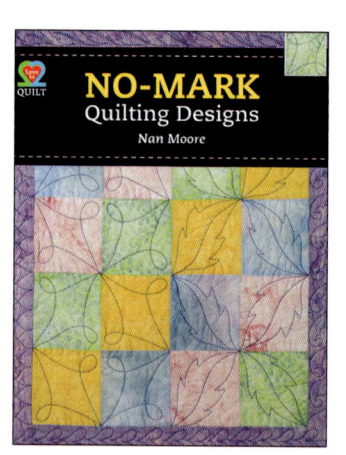 No-Mark Quilting Designs — Nan Moore #1277 .... $12.95
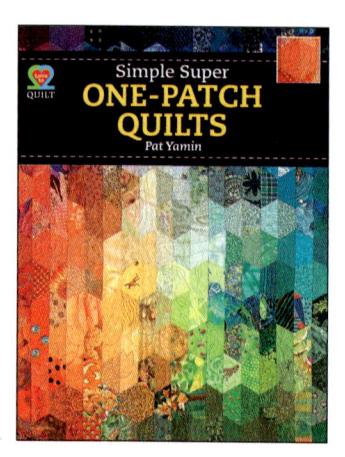 Simple Super One-Patch Quilts — Pat Yamin #1275 .... $12.95	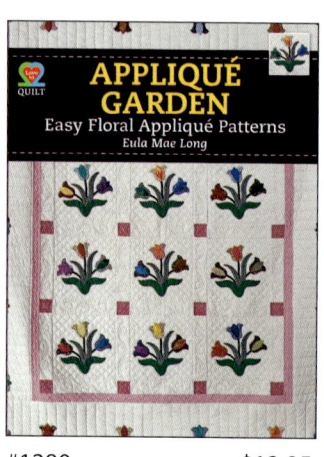 Appliqué Garden: Easy Floral Appliqué Patterns — Eula Mae Long #1280 .... $12.95	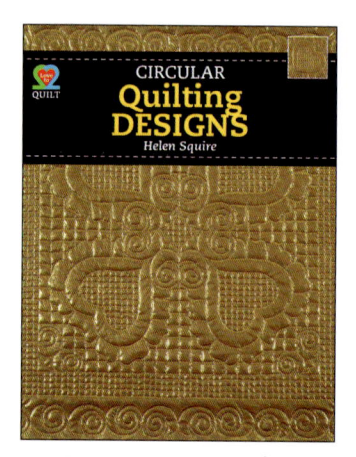 Circular Quilting Designs — Helen Squire #1281 .... $12.95
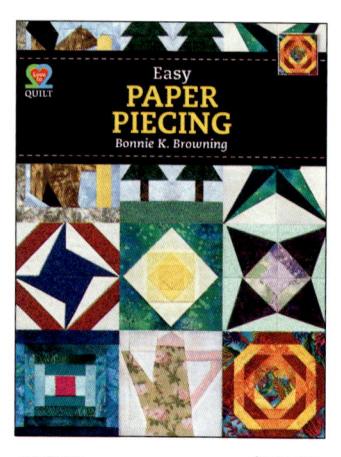 Easy Paper Piecing — Bonnie K. Browning #1279 .... $12.95	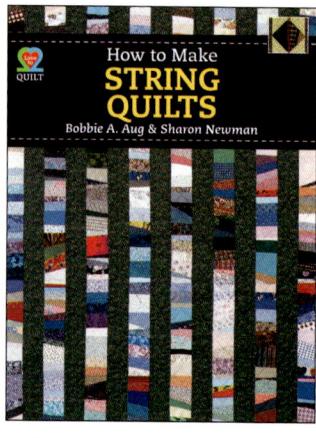 How to Make String Quilts — Bobbie A. Aug & Sharon Newman #1282 .... $12.95	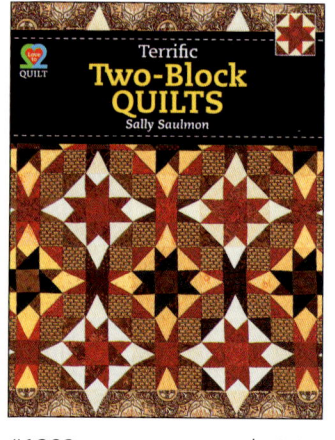 Terrific Two-Block Quilts — Sally Saulmon #1283 .... $12.95

LOOK for these books nationally.
CALL or **VISIT** our website at

1-800-626-5420
www.LovetoQuiltCreations.com